U.S. Fish & Wildlife Service
U.S. Bureau of Reclamation

I0430261

Klamath River Watershed Restoration Program

Request for Proposals

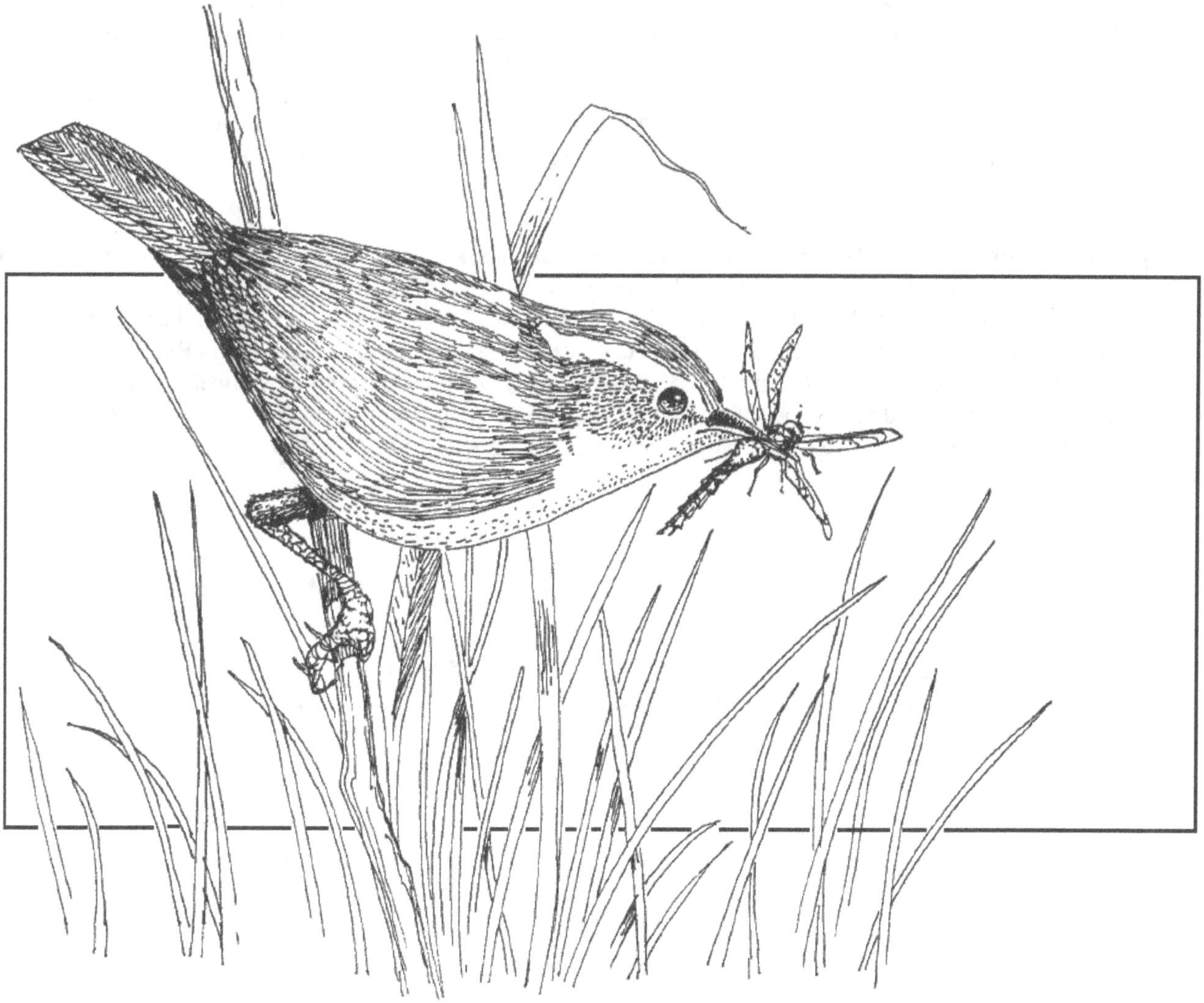

California / Oregon

May 1999

United States Department of the Interior

FISH AND WILDLIFE SERVICE

Klamath Basin Ecosystem Restoration Office
6610 Washburn Way
Klamath Falls, OR 97603
(541) 885-8481 FAX: (541) 885-7837

May 17, 1999

To All Parties Interested in Submitting Watershed Restoration Proposals:

The Department of the Interior, U.S. Fish and Wildlife Service (USFWS) and the U. S. Bureau of Reclamation (USBR) are pleased to announce the Fiscal Year 2000 request for watershed restoration proposals (RFP) in southern Oregon and northern California. Funding is anticipated in four programs including: 1)USFWS Jobs-In-The-Woods (JITW); 2) USFWS Hatfield Restoration Program; 3) USBR Oregon Resource Conservation Act (ORCA); 4) USFWS Partners for Fish and Wildlife (PFW). Each program has different goals and eligibility requirements for funding which are explained within the color coded sections of this application package.

Applications must be received at the Klamath Basin Ecosystem Restoration Office (ERO) by Tuesday, August 31, 1999. Questions should be directed to the ERO personnel; Curt Mullis, Akimi King, Terri Campbell, Sue Mattenberger, Andy Hamilton or Faye Weekley at (541) 885-8481 in Klamath Falls; Paula Golightly or David Boyd at (707) 822-7201 in Arcata; Patricia Bratcher at (530) 527-3043 in Red Bluff; or Laurie Simons, Brie Darr or Darla Eastman at (530) 842-5763 in Yreka. Questions specifically addressing the ORCA program should be directed to USBR, Bob Davis or Mark Buettner at (541) 883-6935. This Request for Proposals package is available on the Internet at: *http://www.kffwo.org/y2krfp.html*

Sincerely,

Steven A Lewis - Project Leader
USFWS - Klamath Basin Ecosystem Restoration Office

Karl Wirkus - Area Manager
USBR - Klamath Basin Area Office

Bruce Halstead - Project Leader
USFWS - Coastal California FWO

Tom Stewart - Project Leader
USFWS - Klamath Basin National Wildlife
Refuges

Dr. Ron Iverson - Project Leader
USFWS - Klamath River FWO

James G. Smith - Project Leader
USFWS - Northern Central Valley FWO

GENERAL INFORMATION

Eligibility

Funding for the restoration programs is contingent upon congressional appropriation allocated to each program. Anyone is eligible to apply for these watershed restoration funds. The table on page 2 summarizes program eligibility and requirements. The color coded sections for each program contain specific information and requirements.

Project proposals may be funded by the following programs:

> **USFWS: Jobs-in-the-Woods Restoration Program - Green Section**
> ~**$670,000** including ~**$100,000** for watershed planning and assessment projects

> **USFWS: Hatfield Restoration & Information & Education Program - Pink Section**
> ~**$850,000** including ~**$65,000** for information and education projects and ~**$100,000** for watershed planning and assessment projects);

> **USBR: Oregon Resource Conservation Act - Blue Section**
> ~**$1,000,000**

> **USFWS: Partners for Fish and Wildlife Program - Yellow Section**
> ~**$80,000**

Your proposal may be eligible for funding from more than one program, but you only need to fill out **ONE** application. If you choose to apply **only** for the Partners for Fish and Wildlife program, **you only need to fill out the PFW form.**

The following table summarizes program eligibility and program emphasis according to project type and geographic area. See the program information sheets in the color coded sections for detailed descriptions of individual program requirements.

	FUNDING PROGRAMS			
PROJECT TYPE	**Jobs-in-the-Woods (Green)**	**Hatfield (Pink)**	**ORCA (Blue)**	**Partners for Wildlife (Yellow)**
On-the-ground Restoration	Yes	Yes	Yes	Yes
Information and Education	No	Yes	Yes	No
Planning and Watershed Assessment	Yes	Yes	Yes	No
Research and Monitoring	No	No	Yes	No
Reduce Drought Impacts	Yes, if project meets other JITW requirements	Yes, if on-the-ground ecological restoration	Yes	Yes, if fish and wildlife benefit
Economic Development & Stability	Yes	Yes, if on-the-ground ecological restoration	Yes	No
Long-term project Maintenance	No	No	No	No
Land Acquisition	No	No	No	No
Cost-share Requirement	Not required; cost-share beneficial to funding approval	Not required; cost-share beneficial to funding approval	At least 50% non-federal cost-share required	Approximately 50% private landowner cost-share required
Geographic Area (see maps on pages 6 & 7).	Non-Federal lands in qualified timber dependent counties in Oregon and California	Klamath Basin, upstream of Keno Dam, with emphasis on projects upstream of Link River Dam	Klamath Basin upstream of Keno Dam	Klamath/Central Pacific Coast Ecoregion

Project Development Assistance

Technical assistance in developing your proposal is available from the USFWS and USBR. We **strongly** recommend you contact the closest office listed on the previous page, for guidance and questions you may have regarding development of your proposal. Discussion of your proposal with the USFWS prior to submission will result in a better understanding of your project.

Submission Procedures

The **Request for Proposals** will be issued **annually**. Your proposal(s) must be **received** by the U.S. Fish and Wildlife Ecosystem Restoration Office in Klamath Falls, Oregon by **August 31**, of each year to be considered for funding.

In order to qualify for fiscal year 2000 funding, your application must be received by **Tuesday, August 31, 1999.** Please submit <u>ONE</u> SINGLE-SIDED ORIGINAL of the complete application.

Send application packet to:

> **U.S. Fish and Wildlife Service**
> **Klamath Basin Ecosystem Restoration Office**
> **6610 Washburn Way**
> **Klamath Falls, OR 97603**
> **Attention: Joni Drinkwater**

Proposal Evaluation and Selection Process

Hatfield, Jobs-In-The-Woods and ORCA

Once submitted, your proposal will be evaluated to confirm eligibility. If eligible, your proposal will be assigned to a field reviewer. Summary sheets will be forwarded to a variety of technical review and planning committees for their information and technical recommendations. You will be contacted to schedule a review of your project, including a site visit. The field reviewer will become very familiar with the project and is responsible for presenting it to the Review and Rank Committee.

The Review and Rank committee is an interdisciplinary group of federal agency specialists that will evaluate the proposals according to an established set of criteria directly related to those items requested in the application. <u>Projects that are not cost effective will not be funded</u>. For qualified **ORCA** project proposals, the Review and Rank committee will submit their findings to the Upper Basin Working Group to make funding recommendations to ERO officials. For qualified **Hatfield** and **JITW** project proposals, the Review and Rank committee will forward funding recommendations to agency project leaders for final selection. Proposals which are not funded through this RFP may be referred to other funding sources.

Partners For Fish and Wildlife

Proposals will be evaluated for eligibility and recommendations will be made by ERO for funding.

Project Agreements and Funding Process

Hatfield, Jobs-In-The-Woods and ORCA

You will be notified in writing whether or not your proposal is selected for funding. Your Project Proposal (modified as necessary) will become the Project Work Plan. An agreement will then be developed between the funding agency and the party directly receiving funding (Cooperator). This agreement is the document used to transfer funds and identify the obligations of the participants.

The landowner and Cooperator(s) may be asked to sign a Watershed Restoration Agreement. This is an agreement among the funding agency, Cooperator and landowner for the following purposes: 1) to establish and facilitate cooperation, 2) to identify and clarify the roles of all the parties in the implementation of the project work plan, 3) to authorize access to the project site for purposes of meeting environmental regulatory requirements, project implementation, and monitoring, and 4) to provide assurances that protect the investment of the restoration effort for at least 10 years. (this requirement applies only to on-the-ground projects). This agreement does not involve the transfer of funds. A sample copy of the Watershed Restoration Agreement is available upon request.

Partners for Fish and Wildlife

If funds are available for your project, a Wildlife Extension Agreement will be developed to fund your project.

Administrative Issues that Apply to all Programs

Administrative overhead must be limited to 15 percent or less. Only project-related costs incurred during the term of the agreement will be eligible for reimbursement. Qualifying in-kind and cost-share contributions must be incurred only during project implementation and must be directly tied to overall project costs. All costs must be supported by appropriate invoices, purchase orders, canceled warrants, and/or other records; including documentation for claimed cost shares or in-kind contributions, upon request.

Environmental/Cultural Resource Requirements and Permits

The USFWS/USBR is responsible for ensuring that all funded watershed restoration projects meet applicable federal, state, and local environmental and cultural resource regulations, such as the National Environmental Policy Act and the Endangered Species Act, **before** project activities may begin. Project work may only be initiated when the Cooperator receives notification from the USFWS/USBR stating that all requirements have been met. If you have any questions regarding these requirements, please contact your nearest Fish and Wildlife Service office.

Landowners and/or Cooperators are required to secure any federal, state, and local land use permits necessary to implement the project, such as Clean Water Act section 404 permits, California Streambed Alteration Agreements or Oregon Division of State Lands Permit. Contact the USFWS/USBR project manager prior to applying for permits to determine if programmatic permits already exist, covering your project.

Meeting all applicable requirements and obtaining permits may take from **three months to over a year** depending on the type of the project and the amount of time required to write the documentation and submit it to the appropriate agencies. Visits to project sites by federal restoration personnel will be necessary to gather information and complete the required documentation.

U.S. Department of Interior Watershed Restoration Program Map

* USFWS : Jobs-in-the-Woods Program
* USFWS : Partners for Fish and Wildlife Program

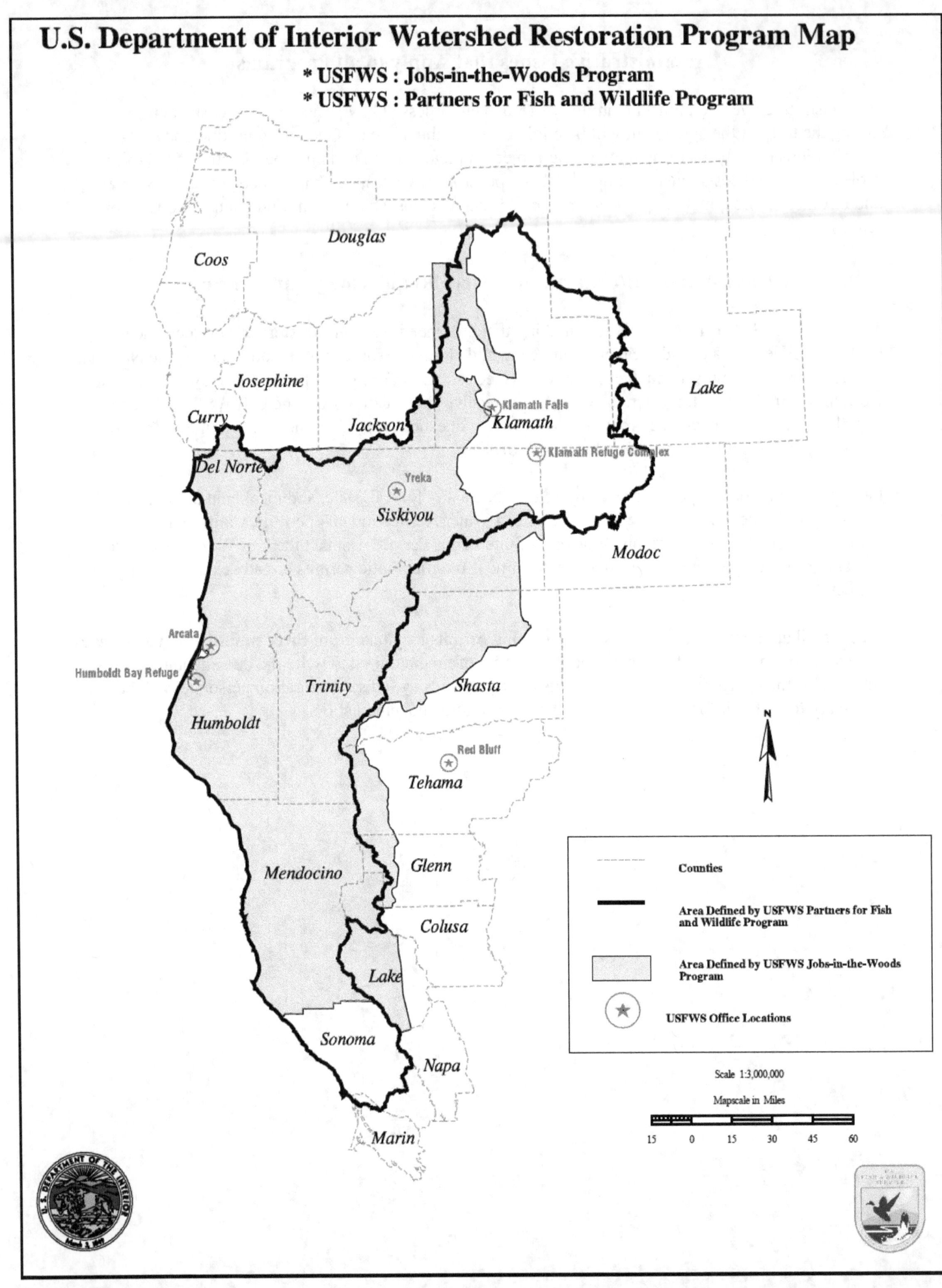

Counties

Area Defined by USFWS Partners for Fish and Wildlife Program

Area Defined by USFWS Jobs-in-the-Woods Program

USFWS Office Locations

Scale 1:3,000,000

Mapscale in Miles

15   0   15   30   45   60

U.S. Department of Interior Watershed Restoration Program Map

* USBR : Oregon Resource Conservation Act Restoration Program
* USFWS : Hatfield Restoration Program

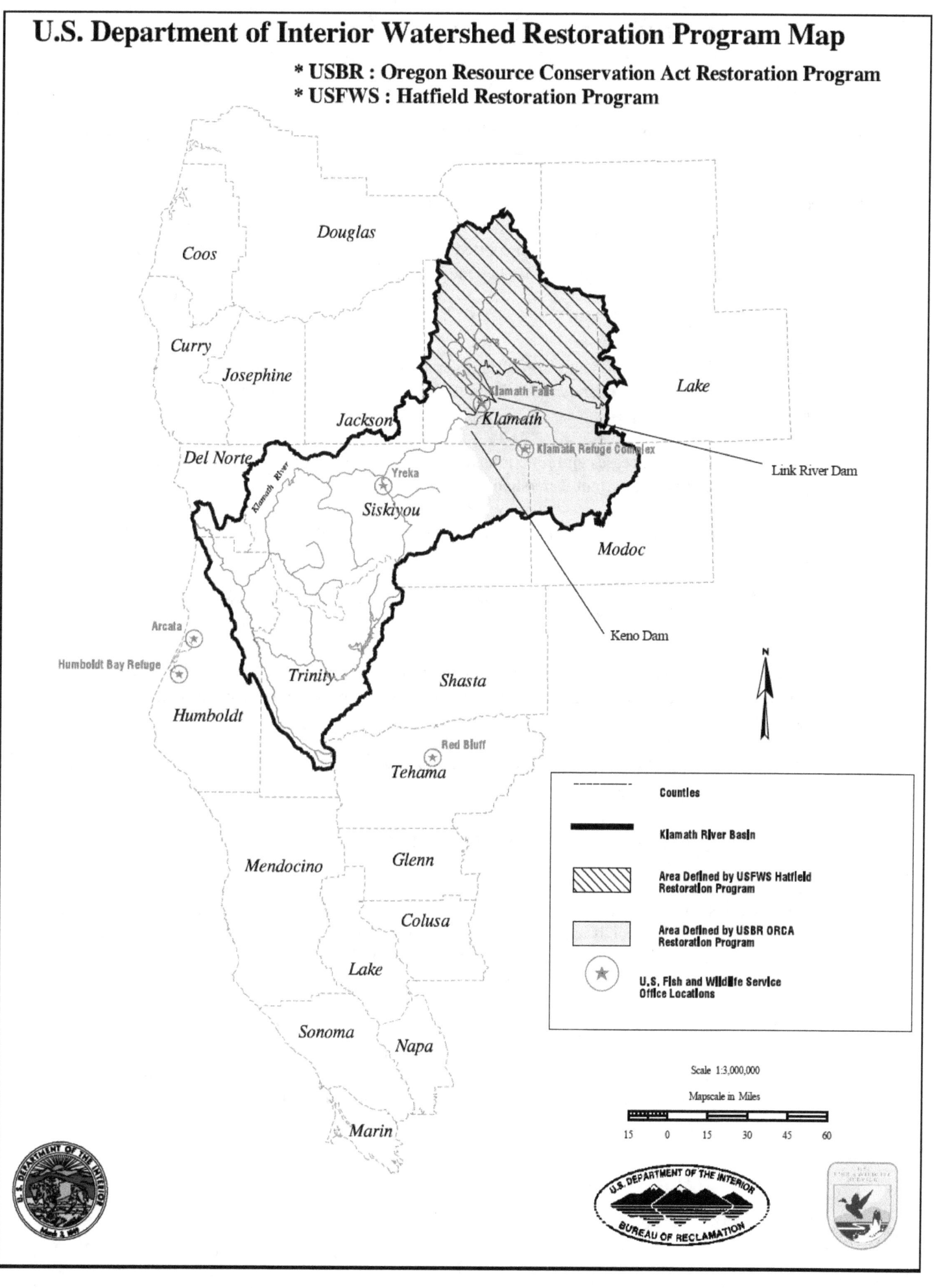

Coos

Douglas

Curry

Josephine

Jackson

Del Norte

Klamath River

Yreka

Siskiyou

Klamath Falls

Klamath

Klamath Refuge Complex

Lake

Link River Dam

Keno Dam

Modoc

Arcata

Humboldt Bay Refuge

Trinity

Shasta

Humboldt

Red Bluff

Tehama

Mendocino

Glenn

Colusa

Lake

Sonoma

Napa

Marin

N

Counties

Klamath River Basin

Area Defined by USFWS Hatfield
Restoration Program

Area Defined by USBR ORCA
Restoration Program

U.S. Fish and Wildlife Service
Office Locations

Scale 1:3,000,000

Mapscale in Miles

15   0   15   30   45   60

USFWS: Jobs-In-The-Woods Watershed Restoration Program

Background:

★   The "Jobs-In-The-Woods" (JITW) Watershed Restoration Program began in 1995 as part of the Northwest Forest Plan.

★   Federal funds were appropriated to the U.S. Fish and Wildlife Service for implementation of a Watershed Restoration Program to support projects on non-federal lands (private, tribal and state lands) within the range of the northern spotted owl. Projects funded are to employ displaced timber workers or workers from timber dependent communities.

Goals of the Program:

★   Restore species composition and structural diversity of plant communities in riparian and associated uplands and wetlands. Contribute to the recovery and conservation of fish and wildlife species dependent on these areas.

★   Restore watershed processes and functions to improve water quality, hydrologic regimes, and the physical integrity of important watershed features.

★   Provide a broad range of long and short-term benefits to riparian areas and associated uplands and wetlands.

★   Benefit economies of forest dependent communities by providing employment and training opportunities.

★   Support and encourage an inter-agency approach to watershed restoration. Promote partnerships with other agencies, watershed groups, and landowners interested in improving watershed conditions.

★   Encourage community outreach and promote environmental education experiences to foster long-term stewardship of diverse natural resources.

Two categories of proposals will be considered for funding:

1) Watershed restoration projects. Approximately $570,000 will be available. Projects, once completed, should be self-sustaining and require minimal maintenance. Contribution by the U.S. Fish and Wildlife Service is usually not more than $100,000 per project, although proposals for larger amounts will be considered and have been funded. Proposals must focus on treatments in one or more of the following categories:

a. ***Road treatments and improvements that contribute to decreased sedimentation:*** treatments may range from full decommissioning to road upgrading. Upgrading may include removal of soil where there is a high potential of triggering landslides, modification of road drainage systems, culvert improvements, and removal or reconstruction of stream crossings.

b. ***Riparian revegetation and associated upland revegetation and enhancement****:* treatment of riparian areas with native conifers and hardwoods is necessary for the recruitment of wood into streams and to provide cover for fish and wildlife species. Revegetation may include planting unstable areas such as landslides and flood terraces along streams, planting wetland areas, livestock exclusion fencing in wetlands and riparian areas, seeding, bioengineered techniques to stabilize stream banks and fuels reduction work.

c. ***In-stream restoration improvements accompanied by riparian or upland restoration****:* treatments may help to improve channel complexity and will be based on the interpretation of physical and biological processes and deficiencies. In-stream restoration is inherently short-term and must be accompanied by riparian and up-slope restoration to achieve long-term watershed restoration. In-stream projects may be an important component of an overall program to restore fish habitat.

2) Watershed planning and assessment projects. Approximately $100,000 will be available. Proposals must identify how landowners will be involved in planning and assessment activities.

Proposals will be accepted for complete and integrated plans for watershed restoration on non-federal land. Proposals must describe a complete and detailed process of watershed assessment that culminates in completion of a plan containing specific recommendations for work to restore non-federal land in the watershed. The proposal must address both watershed characteristics as well as human activities and influences. If public land exists in the watershed, the proposals must reference existing watershed analyses or other planning documents created by the land management agency and identify how activities on the public land influence the condition of the watershed. Watershed plans are to contain the results of assessments for instream and riparian habitat components where appropriate, and upslope conditions beyond the riparian area. This requirement can be satisfied by including assessment activities in the proposal. Assessment activities can only be proposed for the non-federal land portion of the watershed. Results of assessments completed prior to submission of a proposal must be identified and referenced in the application.

Proposals will also be accepted for specific assessments of instream habitat, riparian habitat, and upslope conditions beyond the riparian area on non-federal land where watershed plans have previously been completed. All assessment work proposed must be based upon watershed analysis or planning documents that are acceptable to the USFWS. Examples of assessment work include road inventory and assessment, or collection of information to identify fish passage problems. Proposals must identify watershed analysis or plans which specifically recommend these assessment activities and also show how the results of assessments will be used to identify the need to implement specific watershed restoration projects.

General Information and Requirements:

★   Proposals will be accepted from areas within the range of the northern spotted owl in the following timber dependent counties: Del Norte, Humboldt, Mendocino, Trinity, and selected portions of Siskiyou, Shasta, Glenn, Tehama, and Lake counties in *California* and Klamath County, *Oregon*.

★ Those eligible to submit a proposal include, but are not limited to: private landowners, resource conservation districts, tribes, non-profit organizations, and watershed groups. Voluntary non-federal landowners must be identified to provide sites for projects.

★ Successful applicants and landowners must be willing to maintain the restoration projects for a minimum of ten years to secure the federal investment and pursue habitat objectives planned during the project design. Watershed planning and assessment efforts must include cooperation and coordination with landowners.

★ Projects are to provide employment and/or training to displaced workers or workers from designated timber dependent counties.

★ Restoration projects and watershed assessment activities must be part of a watershed analysis, assessment, or other watershed ecosystem based evaluation for restoring watershed health.

★ Projects must be based on an accurate assessment of physical and biological processes and deficiencies within the watershed. Proposed treatments and designs are to be the most reasonable and realistic for treating causative factors limiting healthy watershed function.

★ Watershed plans and assessments must result in the identification of specific watershed restoration activities to be implemented that will improve watershed function. Sound, acceptable techniques and analysis will be used as the basis for determining the work needed for restoration of watersheds.

★ Restoration projects, and watershed planning and assessment activities are to include methods to evaluate project effectiveness. Projects may also be part of a larger public/private land watershed monitoring strategy for the project area. Determining project effectiveness is critical to determining if identified objectives have been met.

★ Cost share or in-kind contributions are required as part of all proposals.

USFWS: Hatfield Restoration Program

Background:

In 1988, the shortnose and Lost River suckers in the Upper Klamath Basin were placed on the Endangered Species list. A drought in 1992 caused great concern in the local community about the allocation of water for natural resources, refuges, agriculture, domestic uses, and Native American cultural uses and its effect on the local economies.

Former U.S. Senator Mark O. Hatfield established the Upper Klamath Basin Working Group (UKBWG). The focus of the UKBWG is to address ecosystem restoration and water quality, economic stability, and drought impacts. Funding is available for projects which address watershed restoration and improved land management practices (including domestic farm and ranch operations).

Goals:

★ Contribute to the recovery and de-listing of threatened and endangered species with a focus on the Lost River and shortnose suckers.

★ Restore water quality necessary to support healthy riparian, aquatic, and wetland ecosystems in the Upper Klamath Basin (Upstream of Link River Dam).

★ Promote information and education activities which foster long term stewardship of natural resources.

Three categories of proposals will be considered for funding

1) Watershed restoration projects. Projects, once completed, should be self-sustaining and require minimal maintenance.

2) Watershed Planning and Assessment Projects. Approximately $100,000 will be available. Proposals must identify how landowners will be involved in planning and assessment activities.

Proposals will be accepted for watershed planning or specific assessments of instream habitat, riparian habitat, and upslope conditions beyond the riparian. Examples of assessment work include: *road inventory and assessment; identification of fish passage problems; hydrologic assessments; and water quality assessments of non-point nutrient and sediment sources.* If available, proposals must identify watershed analysis or plans which specifically recommend these assessment activities. Proposals must show how the results of assessments will be used to identify the need to implement specific watershed restoration projects.

3) Information and Education. Approximately $65,000 will be available for proposals focusing on information and education activities that promote the Hatfield Program Goals.

Information and Requirements:

★ Proposals may be for watershed restoration projects that emphasize on-the-ground restoration work, public information and education activities, or watershed planning and assessment.

★ Proposals must be compatible with the goals of maintaining, improving, or restoring animal and plant communities of the Upper Klamath Basin. Public Information and Education (I&E) Proposals and Watershed Planning and Assessment are eligible for funding only if they clearly support and facilitate the resource restoration goals of the Hatfield Restoration Program.

★ Priority will be given to riparian and wetland restoration projects that address water quality improvements in the Upper Klamath Lake sub-basin upstream of Link River Dam.

★ Project designs must be based on sound scientific and reasonable techniques.

★ Costs must be commensurate with the resource benefits.

★ Successful applicants and landowners must be willing to maintain the restoration projects for a minimum of ten years to ensure ecological benifits are achieved. Watershed planning and assessment efforts must include cooperation and coordination with landowners.

★ Watershed plans and assessments must result in the identification of specific watershed restoration activities to be implemented that will improve watershed function. Sound, acceptable techniques and analysis will be used as the basis for determining the work needed for restoration of watersheds.

★ Restoration projects, and watershed planning and assessment activities are to include methods to evaluate project effectiveness. Projects may also be part of a larger public/private land watershed monitoring strategy for the project area. Determining project effectiveness is critical to determining if identified objectives have been met.

U.S. Bureau of Reclamation: Oregon Resource Conservation Act

Background:

The U.S. Bureau of Reclamation's Klamath Basin Area Office has been involved with ecosystem restoration efforts in the Klamath River watershed since 1994. The Oregon Resource Conservation Act of 1996 was established to support land owners and managers in improving ecological conditions in the Klamath Basin. The emphasis of ecosystem restoration is to encourage projects in at least one of the following three categories:

Goals:

★ Ecological restoration projects

★ Economic development and stability projects

★ Projects to reduce the impacts of drought conditions

Information and Requirements:

★ Cost share and/or In-Kind Contributions must be non-federal (or qualified federal) and be at least 50% of the total project costs.

★ Projects must be located in the Upper Klamath Basin upstream of Keno Dam, including that portion of the watershed in northern California and southern Oregon.

★ Ecological Restoration Projects must support on-the-ground riparian, wetland or instream restoration resulting in water quality improvements in the Klamath River Basin.

★ Projects must include an effectiveness monitoring plan, or be a part of a larger public/private land watershed monitoring strategy.

★ Monitoring, research, assessments, and information and education proposals must clearly explain how the project will help achieve program goals.

USFWS: Partners for Fish and Wildlife Program

Background:

The U.S. Fish and Wildlife Service has been working in voluntary partnership with private landowners interested in restoring wetlands and other important wildlife habitats since 1987. The purpose of the program is to assist landowners with the restoration, enhancement, and protection of wetland, riparian, and instream habitats. Both technical and financial assistance are available and encouraged. This program was initiated to support the restoration of migratory waterfowl populations, but has been expanded to include projects benefitting endangered species, anadromous fisheries, and neotropical migratory birds.

Goals:

★   Implement and promote habitat conservation on private lands which benefit Federal trust species

★   Provide leadership and develop partnerships necessary to accomplish habitat conservation

★   Educate the general public on the importance of habitat conservation and encourage their participation in these efforts

Information and Requirements:

★   Available to private landowners only.

★   Fish and Wildlife Service contribution to project generally limited to less than 50% of total cost.

★   Limited to on-the-ground projects resulting in the restoration, enhancement, or protection of fish and wildlife habitats.

★   Generally, projects are small to intermediate in size due to the limited amount of funds available.

KLAMATH BASIN PARTNERS FOR FISH AND WILDLIFE PROGRAM APPLICATION

1. Proposer information:

Name:_____

Address:_____

_____

Phone:_____E-mail:_____

2. Location of Project:

Legal Description: T_____R_____Sec(s)_____County/State_____

3. Project Objective:

4. Project Description:

5. Benefits to wildlife and fish habitat:

6. Budget:

Amount Requested:	$_____
Amount Landowner cost-share or in-kind contribution:	$_____
Other contributions:	$_____
Total:	$_____

APPLICATION

Instructions: You must submit your application(s) in the following format. Be clear, concise, and **BRIEF** when completing the application. Please limit your application to no more than 10 pages, excluding appendices and other attachments. ERO staff is available for assistance in project development and preparation of application materials. If you are applying for **Partners for Fish and Wildlife** funding only, use the Partners for Fish and Wildlife Application attached to the end of the yellow section instead of the full application.

1. **Project Title:** Use a descriptive title which identifies the geographic area of the project.

2. **Project Proposer/Organization:** Name, title, address, city county, zip code, telephone, fax, E-mail.

3. **Funding Requested ($):** This is the total dollars requested.

4. **Other Contributions ($):**
   a. **Non-Federal Cost-Share** is a contribution by a landowner, non-federal agency, business, organization, or private individual of cash or labor, use of personal equipment, surveying, or other contributions that would otherwise require funds. Cost share contributions must be verifiable.

   b. **Other Federal Funds** are those being contributed through another federal funding program or contributed in a previous year for the proposed activities.

5. **Location (if applicable):**
   a. **Map:** Include a copy of a U.S. Geological Survey (USGS) 7.5 minute quad, including the quad name, and mark the project location on the map. If your work will occur on a stream or road, mark the upper and lower limits of the project area.

   b. **Watershed:** Identify the smallest stream tributary and watershed(s) where the project will occur. **Example:** *Coho Creek, tributary of the Salmon River.*

   c. **Habitat Description:** A *brief* description of the habitat within the watershed. Example: Second and third growth Coast Redwood and Douglas-fir forest with mixed hardwood species.

   d. **Land Use:** A *brief* description of the land use history <u>and</u> the current land use within the watershed. **Example:** *Historically used for timber production, currently used for cattle grazing.*

   e. **Legal description:** Provide all applicable Township, Range, Section, and Quarter Sections containing the project location. **Example:** *T45N, R5W, S15, SE 1/4 or NESW.*

   f. **Directions to Project Site:** Provide specific directions to each project site <u>and</u> landownership. Permission will be obtained from the landowner(s) before any field visits. **Example:** *Follow Highway 202 south 2.4 miles past the town of Lema. Turn left onto Riverside Road and drive 0.25 miles and stop at the Bridge. The project site is 800 yards downstream from the bridge on the east bank.*

6. **Factors Limiting the Function of the Watershed (if applicable):** What are the causative factor(s) limiting the function of the watershed? Identify probable sources of degradation. **Example:** *Sedimentation of the stream (causative limiting factor) caused by erosion from failure of the road along the stream (source of degradation).*

7. **Project Objectives:** Objectives are measurable tasks that can be quantified. It is important that your objectives address the goals of the program and what or who will benefit from the project. **Example**: *The project will improve habitat for coho salmon and steelhead by decreasing input of sediment to Boulder Creek.*

8. **Does the project address:**
   a) reducing the impacts of **drought**?   Yes ❏
                                                                             No   ❏

   b) increasing regional **economic development and stability**?   Yes ❏
                                                                             No   ❏
   If **yes** to either or both, explain how the project addresses these issues.

9. **Project Description:**

   Is the project primarily:
   > **"On-the-ground restoration"**?   ❏   Complete Part A
   > **"Inventory and assessment or watershed plan"**?   ❏   Complete Part B
   > **"Information and education"**?   ❏   Complete Part C

Part A. <u>**On-the-Ground Restoration**</u>--Project Description and Proposed Treatment: How are you going to complete the project?

1) List the **General Project Category** and the **Project Type(s)** (Appendix A),

2) State the actions to be taken to achieve the project objectives and **quantify** the area to be treated

3) Identify specific **Methods** you will use to implement the actions.

Part B. <u>**Inventory and Assessment or Watershed Plan**</u>--Project Description:

1) List the **General Project Category** and the **Project Type** (Appendix A).

2) Identify what will be done to achieve the project objectives and **quantify** the area to be assessed.

3) **Need:** Why is this work a high priority for the watershed? How and to what extent will the resources and the public benefit? How will you involve landowners?

4) **Problem Assessment:** Identify how you will address the following topics within your watershed where applicable: erosion processes, hydrology, vegetation, stream channel condition, water quality, species and habitats, and human uses. Please reference assessments already completed.

5) Identify specific **methods** or protocols of assessment you will use to accomplish the objectives. Methodology must be approved by the USFWS.

6) Description of Project Products: List specific products to be provided by the project (for example, # road miles inventoried with # stream crossings to be treated and how, # sites where fish passage is a concern and identify how these would be treated, # trees to be planted what species, how and where).

Part C. **Information and Education--Project Description:** Identify specific tasks to be accomplished and how these tasks will be implemented. Include information on the outreach techniques to be used.

1) List the **General Project Category** and the **Project Type** (Appendix A),

2) Need: Briefly identify why and how your proposed project will result in a reaching funding program goals (see Program Goals in color coded sections).

3) Target Audience(s): Identify the group(s) to gain benefits from your I&E effort (i.e. school children, teachers, general public, agencies/natural resource organizations, private landowners, etc.) Include numbers of people to be educated by your efforts.

4) Program Recognition and Awareness: How does your project offer potential for public recognition or build interest by others in restoration program goals. Also include whether your project offers an opportunities for recurrent use of proponents or others (multi-year benefits).

5) Relationship to Other Projects (if any): Identify if and how this I&E project is complimentary to an on-the-ground restoration project or other I&E project.

6) Community Outreach and Education Plan (optional): Describe any *additional* tasks to inform *other* non-target audiences of your project activities (i.e. press releases, newsletters, conference presentations, teacher in-services, events, etc.). Include specific activities and dates.

10. **Applicable Watershed Analysis or Other Planning Document (if applicable):** Identify the Watershed Analysis, Endangered Species Recovery Plan, Coordinated Resource Management Plan, Watershed Restoration Plan or other similar type document that identifies the causative limiting factors in the watershed and the proposed long term restoration/conservation plan. **Explain how the document was used to develop the proposal, and if possible, identify where your proposed activity fits into the plan. Provide a *complete* reference including *Title, Author, Date, and Page*.**

11. **Landowner Participation:**

    a. Provide the name, address, phone number, and fax number of each landowner that will provide opportunities for restoration on his or her land.

    b. Identify whether you already have a signed agreement with the landowner(s) allowing for the proposed restoration project and associated land management and maintenance provisions. Identify any other programs you are involved in, including Wetland Reserve Program or other conservation easement.

c. **Prior Restoration Involvement:** Identify if the listed landowners have participated in previous restoration activities on the property or other property.

12. **Other Partners/Cooperators (if any):** Identify any other partners, other than landowners, and explain the extent of their participation in the planning, implementation, and/or monitoring of the proposed project (e.g. federal, state, city, or county governments; non-profit organizations; consultants; youth groups), and how they will be contributing.

13. **Relationship to Other Projects (if any):** Describe how the project is complimentary (time and location) to other projects? Describe the relationship of the proposed project to any past, present, or planned restoration efforts on, adjacent to, or near the proposed project site.

14. **Land Management Plan (if applicable):** Describe how the landowner plans to utilize the project area for at least 10 years (e.g. grazing strategy in project area including season of use, number and type of livestock, watering strategy; road use or transportation plan for the area; water management regimes for wetland restoration).

15. **Monitoring Plan (if applicable):** Proposals must include a monitoring plan. How do you plan to measure project effectiveness? Please explain how you will determine if the project has met the identified objectives. Is the project included in, or part of a larger public/private land watershed monitoring strategy?

16. **Qualifications of Proposer/Project Designer:** Provide BRIEF credentials and experiences of the project designer. Include information regarding similar projects they have completed. Also identify if you have been a past Cooperator with the USFWS, USBR, State or other federal agency. If you were a past Cooperator, identify you past project and whether you successfully completed the project(s).

17. **Project Schedule:** Provide the projected schedule of events (including instream work periods) from the beginning of the project through completion and submission of a final report. Include the anticipated start date and the projected completion date for all activities. Implementation of projects may be a multi-year process, and we do not expect projects to be completed in the same year as the funds are allocated.

18. **Project Permit Requirements (if applicable):** List all the federal, state, and local permits required to implement your project. Include information on the status of the permits (obtained or pending), date obtained, (or expected date), and permit number.

19. **Community Outreach and Education Plan (if any):** Identify and describe any community outreach/education activities, planned for the project, include:
a) Specific activities and time frames (press releases, newsletters, school activities, training, conferences, events)
b) Discuss how the project promotes or fosters environmental education opportunities and long term stewardship of natural resources.

20. **Employment and Training** (required for **JITW, desirable** for other programs): Describe employment and training benefits of the project. Please address the following six items: a) number of workers to be hired, b) duration of employment, c) worker benefits, d) training opportunities, e) transferable training skills, f) will an Ecosystem Workforce Crew will be employed?

21. **Descriptive Photographs and Illustrations** (optional): Provide photographic prints and/or slides; illustrations, or videos of the project site(s).

22. **Budget:** Attach a completed Budget Estimation Worksheet (Appendix B). Refer to individual program descriptions for maximum funding levels, required cost shares, and other related information. Please include permit costs and personnel time to process documents.

    INSTRUCTIONS FOR COMPLETING THE BUDGET WORKSHEET:

    1. **Personnel** Wages: List wages by position title, number of hours for work on the project, the rate of pay and the total cost for each position.

    2. **Subcontractors:** Identify subcontractors to be used on the project , if any. Identify the position title and the kind of work they will do.

    3. **Materials and Supplies**: Identify the number of items and costs per unit for each line item listed. Include such items as fencing materials, seedlings, etc.

    4. **Operating Expenses**: Identify number of items and costs per unit for each line item listed. May include costs for permits, telephone, travel, etc.

    5. **Indirect Costs (overhead)**: The indirect cost rate should not exceed 15%. Examples of costs to include: rental fees for office space, water, electricity, and other expenses required during implementation of the project.

23. **Project Summary:** Attach a completed Summary Sheet (Appendix C). The summary will be used for reporting purposes and general information. All of the necessary information to complete Appendix C, should be found in your application.

    Note: Please attach Appendix C as final sheet in application package

Directions: Use this Appendix to complete question # 9 (Project Description) in the application.

General Project Categories	**Project Types**
Riparian Projects	Fencing for livestock management/alternate watering Native plant establishment/diversification Bio-engineered erosion control
Wetland Projects	Fencing for livestock management/alternate watering Wetland restoration and enhancement
Upland or Road Projects	Road abandonment, decommissioning, obliteration Re-establishment of historic contours Road drainage improvements and storm proofing Silvicultural treatments Native plant establishment/diversification Fencing for livestock management Landslide treatments Culvert/stream crossing upgrades Bio-engineered erosion control
In-stream Projects	Habitat complexity and diversity improvements Hydrologic regime improvements Coarse woody debris supplementation Landslide treatments Culvert/stream crossing upgrades Artificial barrier removal, modification, creation Fish screens
Watershed Plan/ Watershed Evaluation and Assessment	Water Quality Assessment Stream assessment, road assessment Road inventory and assessment Assessment of riparian, wetland, upland habitats Research and Monitoring
Information and Education	Workshops, educational projects, displays, teacher training Events
Other (Provide a description)	Economic Strategy Drought Relief Other (Provide a description)

APPENDIX B: FY2000 BUDGET ESTIMATION WORKSHEET

	Funding Requested	Other Federal Funds	Other Non-Federal Cost Share Cash	In-Kind
1) Personnel (wages): #Hours Hourly Rate				
Subtotal Personnel	$	$	$	$
2). Sub-contractors				
Subtotal Personnel	$	$	$	$
3) Materials and Supplies #Units Cost/Unit				
Subtotal Materials and Supplies	$	$	$	$
4)Operating Expenses #Units Cost/Unit				
Subtotal Operating Expenses	$	$	$	$
Total Direct Costs	$	$	$	$
5) Indirect Costs (Overhead) _____% (not to exceed 15%)	$	$	$	$
Totals	$	$	$	$
Total Project Cost (add the totals of the four columns)		$_____		

Project Title:

Name, Affiliation, Address, and Telephone Number of Applicant:

Project Objective:

Location:

State: _____ County: _____ Watershed: _____

USGS Quad Name _____ Township: _____ Range: _____ Section(s): _____

Quantification of Area to be Treated: Total Riparian Area _____ acres

Total In-stream Length _____ miles/feet   Total Upland Area _____ acres

Total Roads Treated _____ miles/feet   Total Wetland Area _____ acres

Project Description and Proposed Treatment [include General Project Category and Project Type (Appendix A). For Information and Education proposals include target audience.]:

Employment and Training:

Applicable Watershed Analysis Type Document: _____

Project Funding:		% of Total	Partners/Cooperators:
Requested	$ _____	_____ %	_____
Other Federal Dollars	$ _____	_____ %	_____
Non-Federal Cost Share	$ _____	_____ %	_____
Total	$ _____	**100 %**	_____

Agency Use Only (**do not fill in**):   JITW   Hatfield   ORCA   PFW

For More Information Contact:
Klamath Basin Ecosystem Restoration Office
6610 Washburn Way
Klamath Falls, Oregon 97603
(541)885-8481

Mailing List Update

The Klamath Basin Ecosystem Restoration Office (ERO) is continually updating our mailing list in an effort to serve you more efficiently. If you wish to remain on our mailing list, please complete the following information and return it to the address listed on the bottom of this form. Also please share this with anyone who may be interested in our watershed restoration program. If we do not receive a response back from you, you will be deleted from our mailing list. Thank you for your help in keeping our costs down. You may e-mail us with this information: *joni_drinkwater@fws.gov* or call: (503) 885-8481.

Please print clearly and return this form by June 30, 1999.

_____

❏   Please remove my name from the ERO mailing list.

❏   Please update/add my information:

Name_____
Title_____
Agency/Group/Affiliation _____
Address _____
City _____ State _____Zip Code_____
Telephone (   ) _____
FAX (   ) _____
E-Mail Address _____

❏   To save paper and printing costs, please send future Requests for Proposals (RFP) notices via electronic mail with RFP internet address.

_____

Thank you for your interest in the Klamath River watershed!

Send to:
Klamath Basin ERO
6610 Washburn Way
Klamath Falls, OR 97603